Energizing Sustainability

The Future of Renewable Power Generation

Table of Contents

Chapter 1. Introduction

In an epoch where striving for sustainable environments is of the utmost importance, the future of energy generation portends exciting and transformative possibilities. Our Special Report, "Energizing Sustainability: The Future of Renewable Power Generation" has been meticulously crafted to uncover these aspects in detail. Despite the technical nature of renewable energy technologies, we unravel this topic, making it easily accessible and intriguing for everyone. Whether you're an energy enthusiast, a curious engineer, or simply a concerned citizen, this report acquaints you with the very heart of renewable power generation. Intertwining key insights from scientists, industry leaders, and policymakers, it offers a profound look into where we are heading. Even as we delve into the complexities and challenges of renewable energy, we ensure to remain grounded, practical, and comprehensible. This report not only enlightens but also consistently renews the hope for a greener future. Pause a moment to ponder - the power to foster sustainability is now at your fingertips!

Chapter 2. The Emergence of Renewable Power

Renewable power, once a mere gleam in the eyes of forward-thinking scientists and engineers, has since burst onto the global stage in dramatic fashion. As government policies and public sentiment increasingly align in favor of a cleaner, greener, and more sustainable future, renewable power technologies have emerged as essential elements in our evolving energy mix.

2.1. The Dawn of Renewable Power

The story of renewable power is not a tale of sudden emergence, but rather a gradual evolution, fueled by necessity, discovery, and innovation. The early days of renewable energy were marked by experimentation and exploration, utilizing what could be found in nature to generate power. Waterwheels and windmills were perhaps the first significant forays into harnessing renewable sources, followed by the discovery of electricity and the development of the first solar cell in the 19th century.

The realization that conventional energy resources are finite and their exploitation detrimental to the environment led to the true 'energy turn.' The awakening of societal consciousness towards environmental preservation created a conducive platform for exploring alternative power generation methods. Then, the oil crisis in the 1970s propitiously instigated a worldwide shift in energy policies.

Renewable power sources like wind, solar, hydropower, and geothermal energy began to be recognized as viable options for power production, eventually leading to the development of the modern renewable energy industry. Reminiscent of the industrial revolution in its potential to reshape societies and economies, this new 'renewable revolution' began to gather momentum.

2.2. Technological Advancements

The continued evolution of renewable power generation hinges primarily on technology. As early as the 1950s, the use of solar cells for space missions offered a preview into the potential of solar energy. However, the real drive to accelerate renewable technology development came with the understanding of the environmental impact of existing energy systems.

A torrent of advancements followed: resource assessment techniques improved, devices became more efficient, and large-scale commercial renewable technology became feasible. Wind turbines grew in size and efficiency, and photovoltaic cells saw efficiency gains like never before. Grid integration and storage technologies began to evolve, grappling with the intermittent nature of some renewable sources.

Today, renewable technologies are breaking barriers in cost and efficiency, thanks in large part to engineers, scientists, and industry partners determined to revolutionize the way we produce and consume energy. Moreover, digital solutions are being increasingly employed to optimize renewable power plants, bolstering the efficiency and reliability of renewable energy systems.

2.3. The Policy Push and Public Opinion

Renewable power experienced a swell of support from governments and institutions worldwide, particularly in the early 21st century. Landmark initiatives such as the UN's Sustainable Development Goals and the Paris Agreement have further underscored the urgency of transitioning to renewable power.

Crucial policy mechanisms promoting renewable power include subsidies, tax incentives, feed-in tariffs, and renewable portfolio standards. While these provided early stimulus necessary to initiate development, it's vital that policy continue to keep pace with rapid advancements in the field.

Despite occasional opposition, public support for renewable power has grown tremendously. This is driven, in part, by increasing awareness of climate change. The correlation between public opinion and renewable power is therefore recursive: as support for clean energy increases, policy incentives for renewable energy expand, leading to more research, development, and deployment of renewable power sources—which in turn boosts public awareness and support.

2.4. Challenges and the Path Forward

While the progress has been tremendous, the renewable power sector is not devoid of hurdles. Technological challenges – like integration with existing energy systems, lack of comprehensive storage solutions, and counteractive interaction with wildlife – remain prominent. Furthermore, policy hurdles and market barriers often limit the rate at which renewable technologies can be adopted and implemented.

However, the potential of renewable power as a sustainable alternative to fossil fuels is undeniable. To fully realize this potential, continued innovation, systemic institutional support, and an informed society are required. We are at a critical juncture in the energy narrative, poised with the knowledge, technology, and willpower to tip the scales in favor of sustainability.

A new chapter in this narrative is underway: the emergence of renewable power, a groundswell of sustainable energy that will shape the future of our planet. This emergence is an imperative; not merely a chance at a greener future, but the promise of one. As we embark on this journey together, we bear the collective responsibility to stay informed, act decisively, and contribute to a more sustainable world.

Chapter 3. Unraveling Solar and Wind Energy

Solar and wind energy are two of the most promising renewable power generation technologies. These technologies not only minimize environmental harm but also promise sustainable energy production that can replace, and even exceed, the capabilities of traditional energy sources. Perhaps what's most fascinating is how these two seemingly simple elements – the sun and the wind – harbor such immense power.

3.1. Harnessing the Sun's Energy

The key to understanding solar energy is first focusing on the star at the center of our solar system: the sun. The sun pours out vast amounts of energy, in the form of sunlight, throughout all corners of our solar system. Solar panels are devices constructed with the sole purpose of capturing that sunlight and transforming it into usable electricity.

Solar power, in its most basic form, is simply the conversion of sunlight into electricity, primarily using photovoltaic (PV) cells or less commonly, concentrated solar power (CSP) systems. PV cells, the core of solar panels, are semiconductor devices that generate electricity when they absorb photons, or particles of light. These photons excite the electrons in the PV cells, causing them to flow and create electric current.

This process has no emissions, no moving parts, and requires minimal maintenance, making solar energy a clean and reliable source of power. It's a technology that can be scaled from a single cell that powers a calculator to a large power plant that powers thousands of homes.

3.2. Evolving Solar Photovoltaic Technology

Though solar energy potential is monumental, one of the biggest hurdles has been improving the efficiency of PV cells and reducing the cost associated with them. Over the years, researchers have developed numerous technologies to meet these challenges.

The first generation of PV cells, typically made from crystalline silicon, were quite costly. However, they offered high efficiencies of around 15-20%. Later, second-generation thin-film technologies were developed using alternative materials such as copper indium gallium selenide (CIGS), reducing costs but also decreasing efficiency.

The third and present generation of solar technologies involves a multitude of novel approaches aimed at maximizing efficiency and minimizing costs simultaneously. Breakthroughs in perovskite solar cells and tandem cells increase the possibility of major cost reductions while achieving efficiencies over 25%.

3.3. Concentrated Solar Power

Beyond photovoltaics, Concentrated Solar Power (CSP) represents another powerful way to tap into the sun's energy. This method focuses sunlight onto a small area, typically a thermal receiver, using mirrors or lenses and then employs the accumulated heat to generate electricity through traditional steam turbines.

CSP technologies, such as parabolic trough systems, power towers, and dish/engine systems, can generate high amounts of power, making them suitable for large-scale, utility-level power generation. However, these systems have intensive land and water usage requirements and often necessitate energy storage due to the sun's intermittent nature.

3.4. Capturing the Wind's Power

Wind, a more indirect form of solar energy, also proves to be a compelling source of renewable power generation. Wind is created when the sun's heat unevenly warms the Earth's surface. As hot air rises, cooler air flows in to replace it, generating wind. Turbines capture this wind, and their blades spin a shaft connected to a generator that converts this mechanical energy into electrical energy.

Key factors affecting wind energy production include wind speed, air density, and blade length. Higher wind speeds and longer blades result in more energy production, while increased air density, typically found at lower altitudes and cooler temperatures, enhances energy production.

3.5. Evolution of Wind Turbine Design

Wind turbines have evolved substantially from their humble beginnings. Early designs, such as the traditional horizontal axis wind turbines, were typically designed with a few large blades. However, as our understanding and technology developed, wind turbine design has become more intricate and effective.

Modern turbines are larger, some with rotor diameters larger than two football fields. The greater the turbine size, the more wind it can capture, increasing the energy it can produce. New designs also incorporate more blades to capture more wind, while using lighter and stronger materials to withstand greater stresses.

Additionally, advancements in communication and control technologies have allowed for 'smart' turbines. These can adjust their pitch and yaw to optimize wind capture, providing a more efficient and reliable power output.

3.6. Offshore Wind Energy

An exciting development in wind energy production is the rise of offshore wind farms. While they pose greater logistical and maintenance challenges than their onshore counterparts, offshore wind farms can tap into the powerful, consistent winds over the oceans.

Offshore wind turbines boast larger sizes and higher efficiencies, culminating in a significant increase in energy production. The International Energy Agency even predicts that offshore wind has the potential to generate more than 18 times today's global electricity demand.

3.7. The Road Ahead

Solar and wind energy technologies present a bright and windy path forward for renewable power generation. These advancements indicate that a future powered predominantly by renewable energy is not just a fanciful dream, but a realistic possibility made increasingly achievable by continued innovation. The sun and wind, abundant and untapped, are ripe for the picking and poised to energize a sustainable future.

Chapter 4. The Intricacies of Hydropower and Geothermal Energy

Hydropower and geothermal energy are two of the most substantial renewable energy sources we have at our disposal. Harnessing the potential of these energy sources presents both unique opportunities and intricate challenges. This chapter will delve into the nuances of hydropower and geothermal energy technology, exploring various aspects from their scientific origins to the engineering and environmental considerations involved.

4.1. The Science Behind Hydropower and Geothermal Energy

Hydropower is an age-old technology, exploiting the kinetic energy of moving water to produce electricity. This transition process from mechanical to electrical energy often involves a dam that provides gravitational potential.

Geothermal energy, on the other hand, is heat energy originating within the earth. This geothermal heat is often exploited in areas where geological conditions create hot springs, geysers, or other easily accessible sources of heat energy.

However, harnessing these resources is not as simple as it may initially appear. A multitude of scientific, engineering, and environmental factors come into play.

4.2. Hydropower: Potential and Challenges

Hydropower provides approximately 16% of the world's electricity, showcasing its crucial role within the global energy mix. Yet, its potential is far from fully tapped, particularly in developing countries with substantial water resources.

Crucially, the efficiency of hydropower is markedly high, often reaching 85%. Moreover, it offers a reliable and consistent source of power, with hydroelectric plants capable of dispatching power to the grid rapidly during peak demand.

However, there are numerous environmental, regulatory, and infrastructural challenges impeding the wider adoption of hydropower. These challenges range from environmental and social impact considerations associated with dam construction, changes in water quality, and the displacement of local communities.

4.3. Geothermal Energy: A Glance at its Capabilities

Geothermal energy is an often overlooked star of the renewable energy portfolio. Despite representing a smaller portion of global energy production, its potential is immense—particularly given technological advances in recent decades.

A key advantage of geothermal is its inherent stability and predictability. Unlike many renewable resources, geothermal energy is generally available regardless of external weather patterns.

One of the most prominent challenges facing geothermal power is that suitable locations for power plants are limited by geological conditions. However, advanced drilling technologies offer new hope, enabling power plants to harness geothermal energy from greater depths and in a wider range of locales.

4.4. Innovations and Developments

The future of hydropower and geothermal energy production lies in the ingenuity and innovation of engineers and scientists. There has been a surge of interest in harnessing these resources more efficiently and mitigating the associated environmental impacts.

For hydropower, technological advances are helping to improve turbine efficiency and reduce the harmful environmental effects of dams. For example, "run-of-river" hydropower plants which don't rely on large-scale water storage are proving to be an environmentally friendlier alternative.

For geothermal energy, "enhanced geothermal systems" (EGS) have promising potential. EGS employs innovative drilling and reservoir stimulation methods to increase heat extraction and power generation from geothermal resources.

4.5. The Environmental Equation

Our mission towards renewable energy isn't merely driven by an energy crisis but also by an environmental one. It's therefore significant to consider the environmental repercussions of hydropower and geothermal energy.

While hydropower is emissions-free, dam construction can lead to significant habitat destruction and changes in water quality. Mitigating these impacts requires careful planning and design, and could influence the broader feasibility of hydropower projects.

On the environmental front, geothermal energy is typically favorable. Emissions are minimal, and land use requirements are generally smaller. However, there can be localized impacts including surface disturbance, ground subsidence, and release of harmful gases and heavy metals.

4.6. The Way Forward

There's no silver bullet solution in our pursuit to transition to a sustainable future. Hydropower, geothermal energy, and other renewables each carry their unique set of promises and challenges. As we progress, it's paramount that we strike a balance - maximizing the benefits of these technologies while doing everything we can to mitigate their downsides.

Embracing hydropower and geothermal energy demands a holistic viewpoint, acknowledging not just the intricacies of the technologies themselves, but the delicate nexus between people, nature, and the economy where they operate. This approach will not only power our homes and offices, but also turn the wheels of a sustainable future, for all.

Chapter 5. Fuel Beyond Fossil: The Bioenergy Revolution

The biogenic genesis of our planet has harbored myriad organic forms; over countless centuries, nature has been conducting an elaborate photosynthetic dance, converting sunlight into chemical energy stored in organic matter. Today, scientists and engineers seek to harness this wrapped-up energy, creating technologies designed to convert these bio-resources into emissions-free or low-emission power. Thus, opens the chapter on the Bioenergy Revolution, the future of sustainable fuel beyond traditional fossil-based options.

5.1. Unveiling the Quintessence of Bioenergy

Bioenergy is a type of renewable energy derived from biological sources—specifically, directly from plants, or indirectly from agricultural, commercial, domestic, or industrial wastes. The crux of bioenergy, or biofuel, arises from its carbon-neutral premise: the carbon dioxide released during the generation of bioenergy is balanced by the amount absorbed by plants during their growth. This cycle bestows bioenergy with an environmentally friendly tailwind, setting stage for the creation of a self-sufficient energy ecosystem.

Raw biomass is converted into convenient energy carriers like bioethanol, biodiesel, biomethane, and biohydrogen, each possessing unique characteristics influencing their applications. Bioethanol, derived primarily from sugar and starch crops, is used as a transportation fuel and a gasoline additive. Biodiesel, produced from oils or fats, is a substitute for diesel. Biomethane, tapped from the decomposition of organic waste, is a potential replacement for natural gas. Biohydrogen, although still in nascent stages, could be instrumental in power generation.

5.2. Crop-based Biofuels: Ethanol and Biodiesel

Crop-based biofuels have drawn considerable attention in the initial phase of the bioenergy revolution. Bioethanol, primarily produced from starch or sugar-based feedstock like corn and sugarcane, offers significant GHG reduction potential. In Brazil, known as the bioethanol powerhouse, the sugarcane-based ethanol industry has evolved tremendously, with bagasse, a byproduct, used to create electricity, thereby creating a symbiotic synergy between sectors.

Biodiesel, derived from vegetable oils or animal fats via transesterification, serves as an eco-friendly diesel substitute. The foremost benefit lies in its biodegradability and non-toxicity, not compromising the performance or durability of engines. Rapeseed, soybean, and palm oils make up most of the biodiesel feedstock in Europe, the US, and Asia, respectively.

However, the ethics and sustainability of using food crops for fuel have spurred ongoing debate. Concerns about land-use changes, increased agriculture-related emissions, and food-versus-fuel concerns have prompted research into advanced, 'second-generation' biofuels.

5.3. Second Generation Biofuels: Towards Sustainability

The second generation of biofuels capitalizes on non-food lignocellulosic biomass—derived from forestry residues, dedicated energy crops, and agricultural residues. This offers two-fold advantages: it mitigates the food-versus-fuel conflict and presents a broader resource base.

Cellulosic ethanol, produced by chemically and/or biologically breaking down cellulose in plant matter, exhibits significant promise. Yet, the complex process, high enzymatic and pre-treatment costs, and feedstock handling issues currently challenge commercial-scale exploitation. Similarly, biodiesel produced from algae, called algal biofuel, overcomes land-use concerns associated with traditional biodiesel feedstocks but contends with high cultivation and harvesting costs.

5.4. Towards Biofuel Varieties: Biomethane and Biohydrogen

Biomethane, produced by anaerobically digesting organic waste or via biomass gasification, serves as an eco-friendly alternative to natural gas. Applications vary from heat and electricity generation to use as a vehicle fuel. Beyond mitigating methane emissions from waste, it also fosters waste management and provides a potential revenue stream.

Biohydrogen is another compelling yet initially challenging prospect. Made by biologically breaking down organic matter, it harnesses the cleanest form of chemical energy. The production process, though, is currently hampered by low yields and high costs.

5.5. Policy Framework and Incentives

The bioenergy trajectory is intrinsically linked to global and regional regulatory frameworks and incentives. Incentives linked to the Renewable Fuel Standard (RFS) in the US and Renewable Energy Directive (RED II) in Europe guide the growth and penetration of biofuels. Countries like Brazil have seen large-scale adoption of bioethanol due to stringent blending mandates.

5.6. The Outlook on the Bioenergy Revolution

The plot of the bioenergy revolution is complex, marked by scientific advancements and policy changes. As we move forward, it is the synergy between technology, policy, and sustainability that will steer the path. The quest for more efficient bioenergy technologies underscores the need to orchestrate a global scientific endeavor, one that addresses challenges and optimizes the benefits of bioenergy.

While the promise of bioenergy is immense, the path is fraught with challenges and considerations unique to each regional context. From the ethical dilemma of food versus fuel to land-use implications and emission reductions, the complexities of creating sustainable, scalable bioenergy solutions are numerous. Yet, as society marches towards a carbon-neutral future, more than ever, bioenergy stands as a beacon that may guide us beyond fossil fuel dependency, and into a new age of sustainable energy.

Chapter 6. The Pivotal Role of Energy Storage Systems

The emergence of renewable energy as a viable, sustainable power source has led to some notable shifts in the landscape of power generation. One prominent change is the pressing need for advanced energy storage systems. These systems become crucial when the intermittency of renewable sources like solar and wind is taken into account, which lack the ability to produce a constant stream of energy. While the dynamism of renewable energy sources can be unpredictable, effective energy storage systems ensure a balanced, reliable power supply.

6.1. The Why: Understanding The Need For Energy Storage Systems

The inconsistent, variable nature of certain renewable energy sources creates a unique scenario that poses two important challenges: meeting immediate energy demand and storing excess power for future use. Traditional power plants, operating on natural gas, coal, or nuclear energy, can scale up or down based on demand. However, renewable sources like the sun or wind cannot be "turned up" when demand increases, nor can excess energy generated during peak production periods be conserved for later use without adequate storage systems.

As a result, energy storage systems act as a facilitator for renewable power generation, effectively addressing these challenges. Not only do these storage solutions ensure consistent energy supply, they also allow for energy demand response, providing balance during peak usage times or periods of network instability.

6.2. The How: Technologies Behind Energy Storage Systems

A wide array of technologies are executed to facilitate energy storage, each having unique advantages, drawbacks, and ideal utilizations.

One of the most common forms of energy storage is in batteries, particularly lithium-ion batteries. These products, commonplace in personal electronics and electric cars, offer high energy and power density alongside substantial cycle life, allowing them to store and rapidly release considerable quantities of energy.

Meanwhile, pumped-storage hydroelectricity employs two water reservoirs at different heights. During periods of low energy demand, electricity is used to pump water up to the upper reservoir. When energy is required, this water is released back to the lower reservoir, driving turbines to generate electricity in the process.

Another notable solution is thermal storage, which harnesses surplus energy to heat substances like water, molten salts, or rocks, ensuring this energy can be retrieved for generating heat or electricity when needed.

Further technologies encompass compressed air energy storage (CAES), flywheels, ultracapacitors, and hydrogen storage – a variety which underscores the active research and development in this crucial sector.

6.3. The Prospects: Future Of Energy Storage Systems

With greater emphasis on renewable energy, the importance of energy storage systems will only escalate in building a resilient, sustainable energy infrastructure. Projections posit notable growth in this area, in both the burgeoning evolution of current storage technologies and the birth of innovative new solutions.

Much of this growth will likely be propelled by decreasing costs, particularly in battery storage technologies including lithium-ion batteries. Furthermore, advancements in material science may ascertain the advent of entirely new battery chemistries, harnessing yet unknown elements to store power more efficiently and sustainably.

Moreover, strategies to incorporate plentiful but underexploited renewable sources such as offshore wind and concentrated solar power will doubtlessly drive innovation in energy storage. This could lead to hybrid systems integrating different storage technologies or novel methods for storing energy directly in these renewable forms.

6.4. The Challenge: Meeting The Grid Stability

Storing energy is no walk in the park. It can be quite expensive and complex. For energy storage systems to be effective, we need to consider not just the technology's capability to store energy, but also its cost-efficiency, lifespan, safety, and environmental impact.

Grid stability is another critical issue for which energy storage systems may provide an effective answer. As an increasing number of renewable power plants joining the grid can make it more unstable due to their intermittency, energy storage systems can act as a balancing mechanism. They can provide ancillary services such as frequency regulation, ramp rate control, and power quality improvement that are essential for maintaining grid stability.

6.5. The Role: Carbon Emissions and Sustainability

Not to be undermined is the role of energy storage systems in reducing carbon emissions. By enabling more reliable use of renewable energy sources, storage systems limit the need for conventional power plants, whose operation is tied to substantial greenhouse gas output.

True, energy storage systems embody a complex-structured solution to the multifaceted problem of sustainable power generation. But their utility in this regard is undoubted. By smoothing out the supply-demand curve and enabling efficient use of on-and-off renewable sources, energy storage systems light the way forward in our pursuit of a sustainable power infrastructure. Putting that into context - the larger, holistic goal in sight is not just saving energy but saving the planet.

In conclusion, while the future of energy storage is brimming with challenges and opportunities, it is rich in promise. These systems could be the critical link we need to establish a future powered wholly by renewable energy, ensuring an eco-friendlier and more sustainable habitat for generations to come.

It's fair to say that the pivotal role of energy storage in our quest for sustainability underlines a new epoch in energy – one where storing the breeze and bottling the sun is no longer a mere fantasy, but an approach we strive to perfect. As we stand on the cusp of a green revolution, energy storage systems remain at heart, empowering and assuring, the key to unlocking a truly renewable and resilient energy landscape.

Chapter 7. Overcoming Challenges: Grid Integration and Reliability

When it comes to integrating renewable energy sources into existing power grids, the most pressing hurdle is ensuring the reliability of power supply under all circumstances. While renewable energy sources such as wind and solar are inarguably more sustainable than conventional fossil fuels, the intermittent nature of these sources adds a layer of complexity to their integration with power grids. The grid needs to be operational 24/7, and providing a steady, reliable power supply is an explicit challenge when dealing with resources that are inherently variable.

7.1. Understanding Grid Integration

Before we dive into the challenges and mechanisms of overcoming them, it's vital to first understand what grid integration entails. At the simplest level, grid integration refers to the process of incorporating energy from renewable sources into existing power grids. These grids are designed around the supply-demand principle, meaning that the amount of electricity generated needs to match the amount being used at any given moment. This can be a complex undertaking given the variable nature of renewable energy sources.

There are a few key considerations to ensure smooth grid integration:

- Capacity: The grid must be able to handle the maximum potential output from renewable sources.

- Coherence: The supply from renewables must be seamlessly integrated with other sources of energy to avoid power disruptions.

- Compensation: Mechanisms should be in place to ensure smooth operation in the event of sudden changes or drops in supply from renewable sources.

7.2. Challenges in Grid Integration

Firstly, let's bring to light the key issues the industry faces when integrating renewable energy onto the grid.

1. Variability and Intermittency: The output of renewable sources like wind and solar is weather-dependent and thus, it fluctuates. This variability presents a significant challenge to grid operators who are accustomed to the steady-state operation of traditional power plants.

2. Spatial Distribution: The prime locations for wind and solar farms tend to be remote and far from consumption centers. The transmission and distribution complexities add a layer of challenge to the grid integration.

3. Grid Stability: Frequent changes in supply due to fluctuations in renewable generation can cause instability, affecting the grid's voltage and frequency.

7.3. Solutions for Grid Integration

While these challenges may seem overwhelming, numerous strategies can tackle these problems effectively.

1. Advanced Forecasting: Implementation of sophisticated weather forecasting methods would allow utilities to anticipate changes in renewable energy production. Predictive analytics have been gaining ground in the realm of renewable energy, leading to better preparation for potential fluctuations.

2. Energy Storage Systems: Energy storage technologies, such as battery storage systems and pumped hydro storage, provide a promising solution to balance the fluctuations of renewable energy output. By storing excess energy during peak production and releasing it when production is low, these systems can significantly mitigate the intermittency issue.

3. Grid Modernization: Current electricity grids were designed for traditional, steady power sources. Thus, modernizing these grids to accommodate the unique characteristics of renewable energy sources is a vital step towards sustainability.

4. Demand Response Programs: These initiatives ask consumers to reduce their energy demands at peak periods or when grid stability is threatened. Technological advancement in smart grid technologies has made such programs more feasible and efficient.

7.4. Enhancing Grid Reliability

Coupled with grid integration, reliability is another critical aspect requiring effective management for successful renewable energy deployment. It includes both macro and micro-level perspectives:

1. Infrastructure: As previously mentioned, the remote location of renewable energy sites often calls for the construction of more transmission lines. Building well-connected and robust infrastructure is essential to ensure a reliable power supply.

2. Technological Advancements: Improving turbine technology in wind farms and efficiency of solar panels can improve the reliability of power produced from these sources. Digitalization also plays a pivotal role in enhancing reliability by enabling smarter control and maintenance.

3. Policy and Regulation: Robust policies and regulations serve as a solid backbone for guaranteeing both reliability and feasibility of renewables. Policymakers must ensure that regulatory structures

support grid reliability without hampering the integration of renewable sources.

Renewable energy integration into the grid and ensuring their reliability is indeed a complex challenge but not insurmountable. Achieving this would necessitate a comprehensive and multifaceted approach, including technical advancements, policy-making, and regulatory reforms. With persistent efforts and international cooperation, we can look forward to a future where clean, renewable energy is the norm rather than the exception. This chapter serves as a testament to the feasibility of this vision and hopefully, a precursor to a greener, more sustainable future.

Chapter 8. Decoding the Economics of Renewable Power Generation

Renewable energy, often referred to as clean energy, comes from natural sources or processes that are constantly replenished. Whether it's sunlight, wind, waves, or geothermal heat, these assets of nature have empowered us to envision a future where our dependence on non-renewable sources, such as fossil fuels - coal, oil, and natural gas, can be significantly diminished. So enormous is the potential that it seems to solve our energy dilemmas, fulfill our requirements, and yet, maintain the environmental equilibrium. However, like any other technology, implementing renewable energy at the global level comes with its economic deliberations.

8.1. Understanding the Basic Financial Terms

Embarking on the journey of renewable power generation, it's crucial to grasp some essential economic terms. Let's begin with Capital Cost, which is the money required to build and install a renewable energy system. This typically tends to be high for renewable technologies because most of the costs are upfront.

Operations and Maintenance (O&M) costs are necessary for regular system functioning and typically include repair services, spare parts, and administration charges. These costs tend to be lower for renewable technologies because there are no fuel costs associated with operating the systems.

Another term to note is the Levelised Cost of Electricity (LCOE). It represents the total lifetime cost (capital and O&M) of building and operating a power plant, divided by its total energy output. Simply put, it's the breakeven electricity price that the plant must receive over its lifetime to cover all costs.

8.2. Cost Trends and Industry Dynamics

The renewable energy industry is very dynamic, heavily influencing capital costs. Over the last decade, we've seen some fascinating trends. The cost of solar PV modules, for instance, has seen a dramatic decline, largely due to technological advances, economies of scale, and intense competition in the manufacturing sector.

Similarly, wind power costs have also significantly decreased. Improvements in the design and production of turbines, particularly larger ones that capture wind energy more efficiently, have been driving factors behind this change.

However, these declining costs have often resulted in misconceptions about renewable energy being cheaper than fossil fuel energy. It's important to consider all elements of the LCOE, including capital costs, to fully understand the financial considerations associated with renewable power generation.

8.3. Non-financial Factors Influencing Economics

Critically, understanding the economics of renewable energy goes beyond capital expenses and the LCOE. Several other elements must also be considered. For instance, the renewable energy resource base markedly shapes the cost-effectiveness of power generation. High solar exposure areas or highly windy places inherently favor the use of solar or wind energy. Transmission infrastructure also plays a key role. High transmission costs may offset the financial advantages of renewable energy technologies in some regions.

Environmental compliance costs, yet another aspect, can affect the competitiveness of fossil fuel energy generation. Costs can be incurred for carbon capture and sequestration or for managing air emissions, groundwater contamination, and generation of within-plant waste. At times these are not reflected in LCOE calculations.

8.4. Government Policies and the Market

Government policy plays a pivotal role in promoting renewable energy solutions. Policy instruments can be broadly categorized into fiscal incentives (e.g., investment tax credits), public financing (e.g., low-interest loans), and regulatory policies (e.g., feed-in tariffs).

These policies are designed to either increase the cost competitiveness of renewable energies relative to conventional energy sources or to guarantee a market for renewable energy. However, the efficacy of these policy regimes needs to be assessed regularly on the basis of dynamically changing energy markets and technological progress.

8.5. Renewable Power Generation and Job Creation

An invigorating aspect of renewable energy is its potential to create a significant number of jobs. The capital intensity of renewable energy projects, as well as the propensity to hire local material and labor, makes them valuable contributors to both national and local economies. For example, creating and operating a wind farm requires considerable on-site labor, stimulating local economies in the process.

8.6. Navigating the Risks

While the opportunities associated with renewable power generation are vast, it's critical to understand the associated risks. Market risk, government policy amendments, technology risk, completion risk, operational risk, and credit risk all need to be managed effectively for the successful implementation and operation of renewable energy projects.

In conclusion, as we march toward a cleaner and sustainable future, understanding the economic aspects of renewable energy technologies becomes vital. The trends, the influencing factors, the risks, the policies - these elements shape the economic viability of these technologies. While the road is marked with challenges, the potential rewards of a clean, sustainable energy future and a robust economy are tremendous and make the journey entirely worthwhile.

Chapter 9. Policy Landscape and Incentives: Shaping the Renewable Future

Every country's direction towards renewable energy generation is influenced by public policies and incentive systems. These, in most cases, dictate the rate at which a nation shifts from traditional fossil fuels to renewables. Without the right set of policies in place, even the most abundant renewables can lay unutilized.

9.1. Understanding the Policy Landscape

Renewable energy policy landscape varies from one geographical location to another, influenced by factors such as available resources, environmental concerns, political will, and socio-economic factors. However, there are universally applicable principles that guide the formulation of these policies.

At the core of these guidelines are two crucial objectives - energy security and decarbonization. Energy security entails a continual, reliable supply of energy resources at affordable prices. On the other hand, decarbonization is about reducing the carbon intensity of the energy sector. Achieving these goals hinges on the optimisation of regulatory interventions that include Renewable Portfolio Standard (RPS), Feed-In Tariffs (FIT), and Power Purchase Agreements (PPA) among other schemes.

9.2. The Nitty-Gritty of Policy Mechanisms

Renewable Portfolio Standard (RPS), also known as Renewable Obligation, requires utilities to source a set percentage of their power generation from renewable energy sources. It has been a vital policy tool in driving renewable energy adoption in many jurisdictions. Policymakers set escalating targets over time, pushing utilities to increase their renewable energy capacity continually.

Feed-In Tariffs (FIT) guarantee renewable energy producers a fixed cost per kilowatt-hour for the energy produced. Introduced by Germany, they have proved successful worldwide in driving a rapid deployment of renewables. With FITs, renewable energy producers can confidently project returns on their investments, helping to break down upfront cost barriers.

Power Purchase Agreements (PPAs) are long-term contracts between a renewable energy generator and a power purchaser, often a utility. These contracts contain the terms, including the price and the volume of power to be supplied. PPA's provide an assured buyer for renewable energy, which means they give generators the financial certainty they need to invest in renewable projects.

9.3. Incentive Schemes Supporting Renewables

Incentive schemes are crucial to the success of renewable energy transition. They help to expedite renewable energy adoption by offsetting the high upfront costs and lowering financial risks. Varied in nature, these incentives range from investment and production tax credits to carbon pricing.

Investment Tax Credits (ITC) offer a tax deduction for entities that invest in eligible renewable energy projects, while Production Tax Credits (PTC) provide per-kilowatt-hour tax credit for electricity generated by renewable energy sources. These incentives have significantly spurred the development of the renewable energy sector.

Carbon pricing, on the other hand, is an economic policy instrument designed to reduce greenhouse gas emissions. This can be done through carbon taxes or an emissions trading system.

9.4. Challenges in the Policy Landscape

Despite the increasing awareness and momentum for renewable energy, the policy landscape is replete with challenges. These include technological and market uncertainties, existing subsidies for fossil fuels, and lack of cross-border cooperation among countries. Moreover, maintaining a balance between transitioning fast enough to avoid the worst effects of climate change and doing so in a manner that is economically sustainable is a challenge in itself.

9.5. A Look into the Future of Policy Landscape

Understanding the current policy landscape and incentives is not enough. We must anticipate future evolutions to keep up with the fast-advancing renewable energy technologies. Policymakers have to prepare for an era of energy storage systems, advanced grid management, and electric transportation - all fundamental elements of a future all-renewable energy system. Flexibility and innovation should be at the heart of new policies, not forgetting the competition and harmony among different energy resources.

In conclusion, the policy landscape and incentives are instrumental in shaping the renewable future. Even with the existing challenges, there are countless opportunities to exploit, as long as countries maintain a commitment to pursue this path. The policy tools and incentive schemes discussed can be instrumental in harnessing renewable resources, but the shift to renewable energy cannot be achieved without the resilient pursuit and implementation of these measures. It is upon world leaders to ensure that their policies not only support the renewable energy sector but also inspire innovation and resilience in this vital journey toward sustainability.

Chapter 10. Technological Innovations Pushing Renewable Frontiers

Technological advancement has always been at the forefront of shaping society, and the energy industry is no exception. The sector has witnessed a tide of innovations that are recalibrating the status quo, pushing renewable frontiers, and paving the way for a future underpinned by sustainable energy.

10.1. The Rise of Wind, on Land and Sea

Wind power has swiftly moved from the peripheries to be a frontrunner in the renewable energy sector. Innovations in wind turbine design, including giant turbines hosting longer blades, higher towers, and advanced materials, are helping in the harnessing of wind energy more effectively. Globally, onshore wind now boasts a capacity exceeding 596 GW, enabling nations to power millions of homes in an environmentally-friendly, cost-effective manner.

Over water, offshore wind farms are slowly gaining popularity. Despite the higher upfront costs associated with their installation, offshore wind projects yield higher amounts of energy due to unobstructed wind flow. Technological advancements are progressively driving down these costs and expanding the reach of offshore wind power. A testimony to this is the development of floating turbines, capable of reaching depths hitherto unachievable by grounded turbines, and thus, tapping into the potent wind energy available over deep waters.

10.2. Harnessing the Sun's Power

Solar power technology has experienced significant progress over the past few decades. Economies of scale, improved manufacturing processes, and breakthroughs in solar cell technology have drastically reduced the cost of photovoltaic (PV) panels. Concurrently, power conversion efficiency has markedly improved, pushing solar power into the mainstream energy mix.

Emerging fields like nanotechnology and quantum physics are also playing vital roles in advancing solar technology. Nanomaterials promise ways to optimize the capture and conversion of sunlight, while perovskite cells, a relative newcomer to the solar cell arena, are already paving their way, threatening to disrupt the silicon-dominant market with their commendable efficiency and potentially lower manufacturing costs.

Moreover, Concentrated Solar Power (CSP) provides a solution for one of the major hurdles of the solar industry - power generation after sundown. CSP systems use mirrors or lenses to concentrate a large area of sunlight onto a smaller area. The stored thermal energy can be released for power generation when needed, thereby ensuring round-the-clock power supply.

10.3. Energy Storage and Management

While efficiency enhancements and cost reductions are propelling the rates of renewable energy generation, storage and management solutions are what truly enable a viable shift towards renewables. Energy production from renewables can fluctuate based on environmental conditions, demanding reliable storage solutions.

Battery technology, most notably Lithium-ion (Li-ion), has seen significant advancements. Novel chemistries like Lithium-Sulphur

(Li-S) and Solid-State batteries, while still early in their adoption lifecycle, show immense potential in offering higher energy density and safety features far superior to those of their Li-ion counterparts.

On the management front, the smart grid is a notable innovation. Smart grids use digital communications technology to detect and react to local changes in usage, facilitating efficient transmission of electricity, while also integrating seamlessly with renewable energy sources.

10.4. Bioenergy and Beyond

Bioenergy, derived from organic material, is another promising, under-explored sector. Recent strategy developments are directed towards high-yield biofuel crops, genetic engineering of plants for more energy content, and advanced techniques for converting biomass into useful energy.

One interesting avenue in this realm is the concept of algae biofuel. Algae, with its high yield and non-competing status with food crops, makes for an intriguing candidate for bioenergy production. While still under research and development, the prospect is exhilarating.

In all, as we head into the future, the role of technology in reshaping and expanding renewable frontiers is undeniable. With every advancement, the aim is one - a cleaner, greener, and more sustainable planet. However, it is also crucial to remember that technology alone cannot suffice. Policies, regulations, social acceptance, and funding must align to make this renewable future a reality.

Chapter 11. Looking Ahead: The Potential of Renewable Energy in Climate Change Mitigation

The escalation of greenhouse gas emissions and the consequential crescendo of climate change constitutes an issue of global concern. Within this ambit, renewable energy holds the vital potential to be a game-changer. Expanding renewable energy sources, and reducing reliance on fossil fuels, has significant implications for offsetting carbon emissions and mitigating climate change.

11.1. The Carbon Connection

To appreciate the potential of renewable energy in mitigating climate change, we need first to understand the nexus between energy use and climate change. Energy production, specifically from burning of fossil fuels such as coal, oil, and natural gas, remains a primary contributor to the elevation of greenhouse gas (GHG) concentrations in the atmosphere.

In burning fossil fuels for energy, substantial amounts of carbon dioxide (CO_2) are released, which subsequently creates an insulating effect - trapping more heat within Earth's atmosphere, and leading to global warming. It's this accumulation of greenhouse gases and overall global warming that underpins the progression of climate change.

11.2. Decarbonizing Energy Through Renewables

Renewable energy, sourced from wind, solar, hydro, and bioenergy, emits little to no greenhouse gases during the generation process. As such, an upshift in renewable energy usage could meaningfully decarbonize energy systems and reduce greenhouse gas emissions. This transition to renewable energy can help societies mitigate climate change and pursue a more sustainable future.

We've seen those benefits actualized in various scenarios already. For instance, the widespread adoption of solar energy systems within a single year can result in the displacement of millions of metric tons of CO2 that would have been emitted from conventional fossil fuel-based power plants.

11.3. Role of Technology Advances

Key technological advancements have fortified the renewable energy development - driving down costs, increasing efficiency, and making renewable energy sources more economical and reliable. For instance, there have been significant progresses in photovoltaic technology, wind turbine design, and energy storage solutions. These developments contextualize renewable energy within the ambit of feasible solutions against climate change.

Furthermore, digital technologies such as AI and IoT are enabling predictive maintenance and improved operational efficiency of renewable energy systems. These technologies enhance the integration of renewables into the grid, maintain system stability, and optimize power output - key facets that will bolster the role of renewables in the future energy matrix.

11.4. Policy, Incentives, and Future Outlook

Policy and financial incentives play a pivotal role in the renewable energy upswing. Governments around the world have been increasingly recognizing the value of nurturing renewable energy. Policies crafted to provide fiscal incentives, subsidy programs, and tariff regulations are enhancing the economic viability of renewables.

Investor interest in green bonds and renewable energy financing further bolsters this trajectory, signaling an optimistic future outlook. It's also stimulating industry innovation and adoption of clean technologies - in turn, accelerating climate change mitigation.

However, the journey of transition isn't just a technocratic one. It requires broader systemic changes across energy markets, infrastructures, and cultural norms - a point that necessitates societal buy-in and behavioral change.

11.5. The Societal Aspect

The acceptance, adoption, and benevolent exploitation of renewable energy sources underscore a societal commitment for a sustainable environment. It necessitates empowering societies with knowledge about the benefits of renewable energy and its potential in combating climate change. It also calls for eliminating misconceptions about the reliability and economic feasibility of renewable energy systems.

While the precise contribution of renewable energy towards mitigating climate change is complex, it's indubitable that a substantial focus on renewable energy can contribute significantly to this global challenge. It overshadows the myopic perspective of cost comparison, highlighting the extensive societal, health, and environmental costs associated with fossil fuel usage.

An essential facet, often overlooked, is the role of education and grassroots initiatives. These methods can involve communities directly in renewable energy projects, promoting societal understanding and ownership of renewable initiatives. This community-based narration is integral to galvanizing support and enhancing renewable adoption at a grassroots level.

In conclusion, a future powered by renewable energy presents a model defined by minimized carbon emissions, economic growth, job creation, and a healthier environment. While potential challenges do exist, collective determination and innovative spirit can help overcome these hurdles, transitioning us towards a sustainable, low-emission future. The broad-based benefits of renewable energy present compelling arguments to expedite this transition — underscored by the fundamental call to action for climate change mitigation.